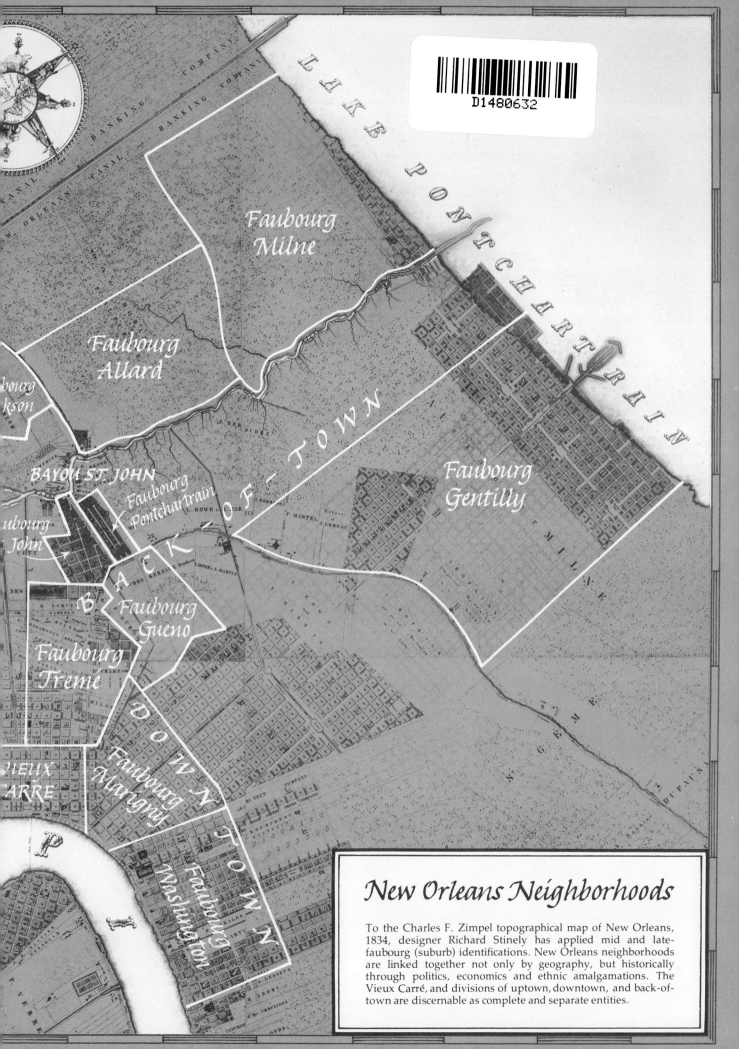

LAKE PONTCHARTRAIN

Faubourg
Milne

Faubourg
Allard

Faubourg
Gentilly

BAYOU ST. JOHN

Faubourg
Pontchartrain

BACK OF TOWN

Faubourg
Gueno

Faubourg
Tremé

D O W N T O W N

Faubourg
Marigny

VIEUX
CARRÉ

Faubourg
Washington

New Orleans Neighborhoods

To the Charles F. Zimpel topographical map of New Orleans,
1834, designer Richard Stinely has applied mid and late-
faubourg (suburb) identifications. New Orleans neighborhoods
are linked together not only by geography, but historically
through politics, economics and ethnic amalgamations. The
Vieux Carré, and divisions of uptown, downtown, and back-of-
town are discernable as complete and separate entities.

New Orleans Interiors

Only two families have owned the Greek Revival mansion in Faubourg Livaudais' Garden District. Built in 1850 for Jacob U. Payne, owner of Barbeck Plantation, the two-story masonry house is renowned for its architecture, and as the historic site of Confederate President Jefferson Davis' death in 1889. The unusually fine interior millwork including the carved wreaths and "lamb's tongue" molding continues throughout the house. In the center hall the mirror, sconces, and inlaid chest are 18th century French embellished with a Baccarat crystal bowl and bronze urns of the same period. Reflected in the Parisian mirror above the drawing room mantel is a 16th century depiction of the Chinese Goddess of Mercy, Kuan Yin. On its shelf 17th century Old Delft garniture rests between French crystal candelabra. A family heirloom, the American Empire table has delicate ormolu swan feet and contains at various times jade pieces, celadon plates, and as seen, a Ming vase.

New Orleans
INTERIORS

Text by
Mary Louise Christovich

Photographs by
N. Jane Iseley

Foreword by
Samuel Wilson, Jr., F.A.I.A.

Published by
Friends of the Cabildo—Louisiana State Museum
and The Historic New Orleans Collection
New Orleans, Louisiana

FOREWORD

by Samuel Wilson, Jr., F.A.I.A.

T HE PUBLICATION of this book on New Orleans interiors by the Friends of the Cabildo, the associates of the Louisiana State Museum, seems fitting for several reasons. First, it presents an aspect of New Orleans not covered by the Friends' notable and award-winning *New Orleans Architecture* series and, secondly, it includes views of the interiors of most of the priceless collection of historic buildings that house the Louisiana State Museum. These comprise the Cabildo, where the transfer of Louisiana from Spain to France and from France to the United States was signed in 1803; the Presbytère, built as the rectory for the priests of the adjacent St. Louis Cathedral but never used for that purpose; the Arsenal on St. Peter Street behind the Cabildo and its adjacent, so-called Jackson and Creole Houses; the Lower Pontalba Building flanking the lower side of Jackson Square, facing its counterpart on the upper side; Madame John's Legacy at 632 Dumaine Street, one of the oldest, if not the oldest, house of the Spanish Colonial period in New Orleans; and finally, the United States Mint on Esplanade Avenue, designed by the noted architect William Strickland in 1835, the latest and largest addition to the Museum's properties.

The Louisiana State Museum, now, with the exception of Colonial Williamsburg, the largest historical museum in the South, had its modest beginnings in 1906 as a result of the Louisiana Purchase Centennial Exposition in St. Louis, Missouri, in 1904. The Louisiana State Building at that World's Fair was a replica of the Cabildo and housed historical, artistic and cultural Louisiana objects as well as natural history exhibits which, largely through the efforts of the Louisiana Historical Society, became the nucleus of the Louisiana State Museum, established by act of the State Legislature in 1906. Since that time, the museum has progressed steadily, sometimes falteringly, its collections constantly growing in size and importance. For the first time, the Louisiana State Museum received the accreditation of the American Association of Museums in 1976, a long sought and highly regarded recognition and a tribute to its professional staff, director and Board of Directors.

To assure continued growth and to work for its adequate financial support and professional operation, the Friends of the Cabildo was organized in 1955 as the associates of the museum, this year, 1980, being its twenty-fifth anniversary. Its volunteers have devoted thousands of hours to the educational programs of the museum, to raising funds for accessions, conservation and other museum functions and to supporting the worthy objectives and professionalism of the institution. The proceeds from the sale of this book will go towards furthering these objectives.

The Historic New Orleans Collection had its beginnings with the purchase of the historic Merieult House at 533 Royal Street by General and Mrs. L. Kemper Williams in 1938. They later acquired other connecting historic properties facing Toulouse Street and established the Kemper and Leila Williams Foundation to conserve their collection of Louisiana historical manuscripts, books, prints and other graphic materials. Since the deaths of General and Mrs. Williams, these collections have been greatly augmented and opened to the public for research, study and edification. The financial assistance afforded by the Foundation for the publication of this book is deeply appreciated by the Friends of the Cabildo.

SAMUEL WILSON, JR., *President*
Friends of the Cabildo

Patios in the Vieux Carré usually separated the main house from the kitchen, *garconnière* (boy's apartment), stables, and servants' wing. Most back buildings were two story, of brick with exterior stairways. Privacy, achieved by the intimacy of buildings and brick walls, is enhanced by thick flowering vines, and graceful fruit and fragrance bearing trees. A tiered cast-iron fountain is the central motif of this lush patio, surrounded by ivy covered brick walls and informal parterres. The two-level brick main house with porte-cochère was built at the banquette in the 1830s. It remains a rare residential survivor in an area presently commercialized by bars and 20th century "street people."

PARADOX thy name is New Orleans.

Founded in the early-18th century by the French, it survived because of native Indians and German-Swiss émigrés. Roman Catholic from its inception, it was secular in practice and known to be tolerant by nature. Semi-tropical and withstanding hurricanes, it also survived repeated freezes.

The French crown, considering Louisiana an expensive, non-productive colony, handed it over in a cavalier manner to the Spanish. Beset with nationalistic pride, the city resisted the transfer, even to the point of open revolt in 1768. Subdued and ruled by the Spanish for thirty-four years, it prospered, but still stubbornly retained its French speech, customs, and building practices.

At the very beginning of the 19th century, if Orleanians were unaware of the importance of their port city, their ignorance was not shared by the President of the United States. Concerned with unknown ambitions of Napoleon and mindful of his acquisition of Louisiana through the secret treaty of San Ildefonso, President Thomas Jefferson, in a letter to Robert Livingston, stated: ''. . . there is on the globe one spot, the possessor of which is our natural and habitual enemy. It is New Orleans, through which the produce of 3/8 of our territory must pass to market, and from its fertility it will ere long yield more than half of our whole produce and contain more than half of our inhabitants. France placing herself in that door assumes to us the attitude of defiance. Spain might have retained it quietly for years.'' Jefferson, the futurist, authorized the purchase of New Orleans; Napoleon, the flamboyant, sold the entire Louisiana territory!

Neither yellow fever epidemics nor the cultural-political differences between the creoles (native born) and les Americains could halt the tremendous growth period that followed the purchase and transfer of Louisiana in 1803. New Orleans expanded from its initial settlement on the banks of Bayou St. John and from within the walls of the fortified city, the present Vieux Carré, to envelop surrounding plantations, known when subdivided as faubourgs. By the close of the 19th century, New Orleans was a city of neighborhoods.

And so it is today. Visitors acclaim the Vieux Carré—the old city—cuisine—its joy and jazz—its most important export. There the parade of paradoxes continues with Spanish patios, American cast iron, Indian gumbo, and black man's music. It is a small land area complete with all New Orleans house types that often display conformity between their architecture and interior furnishings. It is the center from which all the neighborhoods extend.

It was here, facing the crescent of the Mississippi river, that French-Canadian Jean Baptiste Le Moyne, Sieur de Bienville, established New Orleans in 1718, naming it for the powerful Philippe, Duc d'Orléans, regent for the young Louis XV.

Three years later French military engineers LeBlond de la Tour and Adrien de

Brick creole cottages covered with ship-lap boards, 1844 by Louis Surgi.

Pauger, following the military traditions of Vauban, made a formal plan for the city. It became the capital of the entire Louisiana territory, a land mass reaching from the shores of the Gulf of Mexico to the Canadian border—almost fifteen present states.

Streets were laid out in a grid pattern and were named for nobles of the royal family. The same designations remain today, with similar honors bestowed on Bienville, his brother Iberville, and the Ursulines (nuns who came in 1726). The French barracks are recalled in the last street before Esplanade, a military boundary of the old city, similar to its ramparts. Situated where a fort once stood, Rampart Street intersects with Canal Street, a wide space reserved by the French for a canal that was never dug.

Jackson Square, evolved from the Place d'Armes and the Plaza de Armas, glorifies the memory of General Andrew Jackson, who saved the city from the invading British in the Battle of New Orleans in January, 1815. That the peace treaty had been signed by the Americans and English almost a month before the battle did not diminish the gratitude of New Orleans. Peace or no peace, what the English might have done with New Orleans and Louisiana had they won the battle has always been the subject of historical speculation.

In the center of the square, a bronze equestrian statue by Clark Mills of the victorious Jackson was erected in 1856. On its base General Benjamin "Spoons" Butler, at the fall of New Orleans in 1862, inscribed one of Jackson's quotes: "The Union must and shall be preserved." Jackson Square is surrounded on three sides by buildings reflecting both the foreign domination of the city and the newer Anglo-American style.

The Cabildo, formerly the city hall, was designed by French-born architect Gilberto Guillemard in 1795, and is strongly reminiscent of Spanish Cabildos in Cuba, Peru, and Mexico. Its twin, the Presbytère, begun first as the Cathedral rectory, was not completed until 1813. Both buildings were two-story, with flat roofs and balustrades, and both are presently museums.

The Baroness Micaëla Pontalba, daughter of Spaniard Don Andrés Almonester y Rojas and creole Louise de la Ronde, successively employed two Irish architects in 1850, James Gallier, Sr. and Henry Howard, to design row houses along each side of Jackson Square. Anticipating the "Pontalba Blocks" the city added third floor mansard roofs to the Cabildo and Presbytère, thus producing symmetry of height among the buildings. While using Philadelphia red brick and New York cast iron, the baroness's project was intended to recreate the atmosphere of the Palais Royal in Paris.

The St. Louis Cathedral, prominent in its central position between the Cabildo and the Presbytère, was designed by French architect Jacques N. B. de Pouilly in 1850, and was constructed by Irish builder Patrick Kirwan. It is essentially the third church on the site and its scale rather than style gives it harmony with its neighbors.

Along the narrow streets of the French Quarter are glaring architectural opposites reflecting the long period of their development. Rows of buildings that are placed on small, deep lots, directly on the banquette or sidewalk, often share common walls, and through their proportions give the illusion of space and similarity of style.

Madame John's Legacy near Jackson Square was built in 1788 by an American for a Spanish owner in French West Indian style. It stands near creole cottages, an architectural type inherited from early French-Canadian and Mediterranean settlers, and also near the side-hall American townhouses deplored by English-born American architect B.H.B. Latrobe: ". . . that altho the sort of house built here by the French is not the best specimen of French arrangement, yet is it infinitely, in my opinion, superior to that arrangement which we have inherited from the English. But so inveterate is the habit that the merchants from the old United States, who are daily gaining ground on the manners, the habits, the opinions, and the domestic arrangements of the French, have already begun to introduce the detestable, lopsided, London house. . . The old English side-passage house with the stairs at the end . . . is taking the place of the French porte-cochère. In Faubourg St. Mary and wherever the Americans build, they exhibit their flat brick fronts with a sufficient number of holes for light and entrance."

While welcoming thousands of French-speaking refugees from Saint Domingue, both white and free persons of color, most of the creoles of the city opposed the influx of Americans, particularly the flatboatmen from Kentucky, and the aggressive businessmen from the eastern seaboard. There had been bursts of financial advancement during both the French and Spanish colonial periods, but true change, accompanied by massive waves of immigration, occurred after the Louisiana Purchase.

Plantation and country seats were subdivided downriver and upriver of the original city. Soon behind the town, or back-of-town, toward Bayou St. John, scores of faubourgs (suburbs) were developed. During the 19th century, as neighborhoods flowed from one into the other, simple labeling such as uptown, downtown, and back-of-town gave broad definition.

Within these inclusive divisions, individual faubourgs such as Marigny and New Marigny were surveyed and lots sold, as early as 1805. Bernard de Marigny, descendant of an illustrious French family, would not sell his downtown land to arriving Americans. The prediction by an irate American that he would see rank grass fill the streets of the new suburb became a temporary reality. Faubourgs Marigny and New Marigny awaited significant development until the 1830s and 1840s. When the buildings came, they were retardate in style, reproducing French types with Anglo-American ones. Marigny is a compact, intimate section, but more complicated in layout than the French Quarter because of the abrupt bending of its narrow streets.

Further downriver, or downtown, as far as the Orleans-St. Bernard Parish (county) line, Faubourgs Daunoy, Montegut, Montreuil, and Clouet, also subdivided in the early-19th century, awaited a post-Civil War development. The 1834 Jackson Barracks is a rare survivor from an earlier time.

Behind the Vieux Carré, the back-of-town lands of Claude Tremé, a French émigré in the Spanish period, flourished from the time of their purchase by the city in 1810. Tremé was the first municipally subdivided faubourg; all other plantations had heretofore been surveyed at the request of original owners and real estate promoters. In Faubourg Tremé, contracts were let by major entrepreneurs, the French-speaking free people of color, many from Saint Domingue, to construct hundreds of creole cottages.

These were in every form: galleried and ungalleried, dormered and dormerless. They were set back in large properties and called *maison principale,* placed directly on the banquette or on the corners as stores, with double-pitched roofs and sidewalk *abat-vents* (wind and sun covers). These house types very often appear to be frame, but most often are constructed of brick between posts and covered with beaded or ship-lap boards.

Prior to the prolongation of Esplanade Avenue from the Mississippi River to Bayou St. John, only the high land of an ancient portage provided a link between the Vieux Carré, Tremé, and bayou faubourgs, Pontchartrain and St. John. Roughly paralleling this *Chemin du Bayou,* Esplanade Avenue after almost forty years of spasmodic negotiations, was cut through thirty former plantations to reach its Bayou St. John terminus.

Settlement of the area around this important bayou had begun even before Bienville founded the city of New Orleans. While the importance of New Orleans as a port is due to its location on the Mississippi River, in its early days much of the city's commerce passed from the Gulf of Mexico through Lake Pontchartrain to Bayou St. John.

French naturalist C. C. Robin commented upon his arrival in New Orleans:

". . . the entrance of Bayou St. John [at Lake Pontchartrain] is guarded by a fort. The defense is not difficult. . . The land through which it [the bayou] passes in its multiple windings is everywhere flooded by the water of the stream and lake; . . . These stagnant waters swarm with reptiles, especially alligators. . . They are shaded by tall trees which are, however, crowded and deformed and covered from their tops to the ends of their branches with a lugubrious covering of a plant parasite, a kind of greyish moss, which hangs down in festoons up to seven feet long. This covering conceals most of the foliage and gives to these wild places a strange air of sadness. As one proceeds, however, the land gradually rises and soon is high enough to be inhabited . . . and one sees here and there the handsome houses of the countryside. They are of the most varied form—some built of wood, surrounded by galleries in the Chinese fashion, others built of brick are surmounted by a gallery in the Italian manner. Several have colonnades and there are among them some that would do credit to the suburbs of Paris. All of them have a garden in front. Avenues of magnificent orange trees can be seen. . ."

No longer stagnant or a harbor for alligators, Bayou St. John still flows to the lake, bordered on one side by playing fields and golf courses of City Park, and on the other by 20th century homes. Near the Esplanade Avenue bridge and the entrance to Grand Route St. John, the location of the "ancient portage," there are several homes similar to those seen by Robin in 1803.

The Americans, for the most part unwelcomed in the creole faubourgs, crossed Canal Street to build a new city in Faubourg Ste Marie. First came raised plantation homes with spacious gardens, then creole cottages, then rows of warehouses to store the trade items from a burgeoning river commerce.

With the extension of mercantile ventures, commodious homes gave way to brick townhouses and buildings combining residential and commercial usage. These were placed at the banquette with patios in the rear, thus emulating the French Quarter conservation of space. This was the only similarity with the Vieux Carré, for an Anglican architectural tradition of three-bay, side-hall structures had been firmly introduced!

The builder-architects of Faubourg Ste Marie, designed to become New Orleans Central Business District and American Sector, were themselves immigrants from Ireland, Scotland, and England. They had participated in the design of Grosvenor Estate in London, Mountjoy Square in Dublin, and the remodelings of 18th century Bath and Edinburgh. James Gallier, Sr., Henry Howard, Samuel Jamison, Lewis Reynolds, and the Dakin brothers were the men who through ambitious commissions were responsible for much of the district.

Long before Faubourg Ste Marie, equivalent in size to the old city, was filled to capacity, the Americans continued their uptown expansion. One after the other, former riverfront plantations and faubourgs were digested into neighborhoods. A steady stream of immigrants in the 1820s, 1830s, and 1840s—recruited to dig major navigational canals, build railroads, and improve an antiquated road system— required housing.

For these German and Irish immigrants, American entrepreneurs built inexpensive creole cottages and double-level houses, the tall façades of which are reminiscent of a Western movie set. Their own mansions were situated nearby; their riverfront businesses punctuated both.

Many years later this area of Faubourgs Delord, Saulet, and Annunciation (Nuns) became known as the Lower Garden District. Tucked comfortably between uptown Faubourg Livaudais, later the Garden District, and Faubourg Ste Marie, the Lower Garden District was a semi-urban aggregation of mansions, rental houses, commercial buildings, shops, churches, and saloons—all essential elements for a complete New Orleans neighborhood!

For the first time since the Bayou St. John settlement, gardens were planted in front and along the sides of houses. Emphasis, unlike the French manner, was on the front and side elevations, where double galleries and ornate doorways were

Creole cottage fourplex next to a double two-story frame house with rusticated façade, 1850, L. Reizenstein.

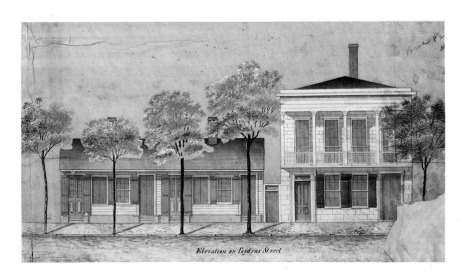

Elevation on Paydras Street

highlighted. Streets were named to suit the fancy of Bathélémy Lafon, the surveyor, whose choices from mythology were: Coliseum, Melpomene, Euterpe, Nyades—the latter became St. Charles Avenue.

The march of Americans was halted both upriver and downriver by faubourgs in the possession of creoles, who in the 1820s were uninterested in the expansion of New Orleans. Then in 1832, Mme Jacques Esnold Dugué de Livaudais, living in Paris, succumbed to a handsome offer of $500,000, and sold to some enterprising Americans the plantation received in a divorce settlement. Mme Livaudais was the daughter of Philippe de Marigny and sister of Bernard, both of whom were reported to be among the wealthiest men in America.

The purchasers wasted no time in engaging surveyor Benjamin Buisson to subdivide the plantation. This land and neighboring Faubourg Panis up to Faubourg Wiltz were incorporated into their own municipality, the City of Lafayette, in 1833. It became a bustling riverfront city. A sea captain noted a few years later: "Streets are piled in every direction with mounds of cotton, which rise as high as the roof; storehouses are bursting with bales, steam and hydraulic presses hiss at your every tenth step." Competition with New Orleans was inevitable. In order to avoid conflict, and to maintain a spirit of progress, the City of Lafayette in 1852 joined New Orleans.

From that time, large homes with luxurious gardens were established in great profusion. All of the houses were set back, surrounded by verdant lawns, flowering trees, and ancient oaks. Many of the Lower Garden District residents moved into the Garden District, but the strong Irish-German population occupying the riverfront land in both the lower and upper Garden Districts remained stable property owners and renters until after World War II. There is no German section of the city, and the specific area known as the Irish Channel defies absolute identification. Many conclude that it is a cluster of streets between the riverfront and Magazine Street in the former Faubourg of the Nuns.

The next upriver municipality, the City of Jefferson, linked seven former faubourgs. Prior to its incorporation in the 1850s, the individual plantations were Plaisance, Delachaise, St. Joseph, East and West Bouligny, Avart, and Rickerville. Most of the sections were subdivided already, and family names and surnames

Rusticated masonry side-hall Garden District house with chimneyed gables and an Italianate bay, 1870 by J. A. Cellas.

applied to the faubourgs and their streets. The daughters of Samuel Ricker and the executor of his estate, Samuel J. Peters, ordered the division of their land into Rickerville in 1849, naming streets Leontine, Octavia, and Peters.

Plaisance and St. Joseph were exceptions. The former subdivided in 1807, was called Quartier Plaisance after a community in Saint Domingue, and the latter honored St. Joseph, a patron saint of Louis Avart. On the other hand, the Faubourgs Bouligny were developed by Laurent Millaudon and Samuel Kohn, two real estate promoters who, recognizing the revival of interest in everything French in the 1830s, gave the names of Napoleon's victories to most of the Bouligny streets. The main thoroughfare was reserved to honor the great general himself. Benjamin Buisson, the surveyor, was incidentally, an officer in Napoleon's army.

Jefferson City became part of New Orleans during the Reconstruction year of 1870. It was a completely rural area until the World's Industrial and Cotton Centennial Exhibition in 1884, at which time Victorian frame houses began to mushroom. One of the borders of Jefferson City, St. Charles Avenue, represents the early-20th century and a boom period in stone mansions of various neoclassical revival types.

Hurstville, Bloomingdale, Burtheville, along with Faubourg Foucher, and Greenville, today comprise the University Section of New Orleans. St. Mary's Dominican College, Tulane University, and Loyola University are within a four block radius of one another and dominate the area. These five faubourgs lying between Jefferson City and their upriver neighbor, Carrollton, were never incorporated into either. When Carrollton was annexed to New Orleans in 1874, these faubourgs were taken in also.

The municipality of Carrollton was formed in 1833. General William Carroll bivouacked there on the plantation of Jean Baptiste McCarty eighteen years earlier on his way to join General Andrew Jackson for the Battle of New Orleans. His renown and presence have been offered as an explanation for the name of the community. An alternative theory is that developers Laurent Millaudon, Samuel Kohn, and John Slidell, whose paramount interest was to build a railroad to the area, aided their cause by naming the municipality for Charles Carroll, last surviving signer of the Declaration of Independence and a great promoter of railroads. He died the year that Carrollton was founded, and his fame was acclaimed broadly throughout the nation.

German surveyor Charles Zimpel laid out Carrollton, and in 1852 it became the seat of Jefferson parish government. The Carrollton Hotel, built by the New Orleans and Carrollton railroad in 1833 at the river's bend, provided everyone with a popular resort with beautiful gardens, excellent cuisine, and a delightful spot for *les fêtes champêtres*. It prospered until 1891, long after Carrollton had become the last of the upriver neighborhoods to be incorporated into New Orleans.

Each neighborhood within the city has a predominant house or building type, yet most are composites of many popular types and styles. Creole cottages, so-called because they originated in the earliest neighborhoods, afford adequate living space with four

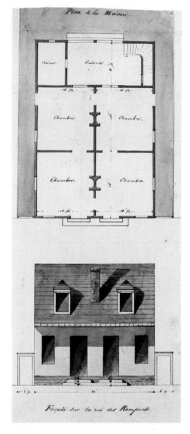

Creole cottage showing four-room floorplan with *cabinet* gallery, 1842 by Jacques de Pouilly.

square rooms. Most have open galleries with small enclosed rear closets known as *cabinets*. One of the *cabinets* was sometimes reserved for a small curving stairway leading to a dormered attic. Separate buildings or dependencies provided kitchen and servants' quarters.

This same plan was enlarged to six rooms with front and rear galleries, still without halls, but raised on brick piers to avoid flooding and maximize air circulation. New Orleans high water table prohibits basements below the ground, so that these raised spaces below the main floor were often left unfinished and utilized for storage. As the dimensions of these houses grew, the roof was hipped, and in the French manner, canted. A center hall, primarily Georgian in inspiration, was incorporated; the houses became known as raised villas and were most prevalent in the Garden District throughout the mid and late-19th century.

The shotgun, a term attached to the architectural vocabulary of New Orleans, may well have an African origin. Historians claim that in 1810, when blacks outnumbered whites in New Orleans, the shotgun became a solution to inexpensive housing and gave expression to a familiar Haitian type. It is found in both rural and urban areas throughout the south and as far north as Canada. A front gabled roof covers one, two, or as many as five rooms, situated *ensuite* (one behind the other) on narrow lots. It is said that if the front door were opened a glance or a shot could be fired to the rear without hitting a partition.

The shotgun is adaptable. A variant popular with all neighborhoods, except Faubourg Ste Marie, is the shotgun double—two singles, but under a common roof. When enlarged vertically with a two-story section attached to the rear, they are known as "camelbacks."

Galleried, Greek Revival shotguns dating from the 1850s are particularly noted in the Lower Garden District and Garden District. Brackets and decorations of turned wood, combined with Italianate features, supply these structures with diversity; when placed in multiples and rows, they give street after street a delightful rhythm of repetition.

To the basic New Orleans house types—the creole cottage, the side-hall and center-hall, and the shotgun—were added Greek Revival, Italianate, and eclectic styles. Few Gothic houses were ever built in New Orleans, but late-Victorian and turn-of-the-century Queen Anne Revival homes proliferated in the Old City of Jefferson, the University Section, and Carrollton. The interiors of these houses usually reflected furnishings harmonious with the house type.

Greek Revival frame shotgun, 1857 by J. H. Mundy.

Heavily carved furniture, deep reds and other vibrant colors, gas-light chandeliers, all conjure a picture of New Orleans interiors. The image accurately represents the decorative selections of the 1840s and 1860s. Two French-born cabinetmakers, François Seignouret and Prudent Mallard working then with rich rosewood, inlaid it with lemonwood, and produced quantities of massive bedroom, dining, and living room suites. Together they created the "New Orleans Look."

Prior to that period, New Orleanians, as inventories from the 18th and 19th centuries attest, had in great abundance armoires, chairs, and tables. The type of wood was sometimes men-

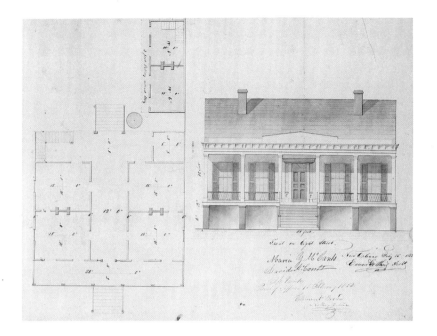

Center-hall raised villa with rear stairway *cabinet,* 1853 by Edward Gottheil.

tioned, but the only indication of style appeared with an occasional reference to *pied de biche* (doe foot).

In one of the earliest inventories, that of the Duvernay Concession in 1726, the only furniture listed was two large kitchen tables, two benches, both of wood, and one cupboard fitted with cloth. Great quantities of table linens, both coarse and handworked, were ever present inventory items throughout both centuries, as were brass and yellow copper candleholders.

In 1769, when Jean Baptiste Prevost died, his inventory indicated furniture and effects of greater refinement. The amazing number of fifty or more cane or rush chairs, both armchairs and side ones, was counted; whereas, only one large armchair, ''back upholstered in damask,'' was included. Several cane settees, probably Louisiana-made, were listed along with items that were very likely imported: a marble-top table on a gilded pedestal, a marquetry one, and another of walnut with a marble top. A clock with brass ornaments, large gilt-framed mirrors with crests, mantle sconces—two with enameled flowers and two others of whitened brass—and several tapestries of painted linen, along with red plush *portières* (draperies over door hangings), give ample evidence of lovely room appointments. In the bedrooms each walnut bedstead had doe foot designs, testers, calico coverlets, lawn mosquito nets, and green serge curtains. Whether an actual bed alcove was built into the room is not known, but the bed area had its own night table, tapestry, and green serge alcove curtains.

There were cypress, walnut, cedar, and baywood armoires and chests of drawers of walnut, some ornamented, some not. Delft and porcelain plates, a goodly supply of silver flatware and serving dishes, as well as a mass of kitchen items, add to the richness of the family possessions. Equally revealing, however, is the indication of the color scheme. At least twenty-four chairs and several settees were said to have covers of red and blue Utrecht velvet. A *lit de repos* (daybed) covered in gingham and quilted bed coverlets suggest color. Unfortunately the theme of the tapestries and their colors were omitted.

The quest for information concerning Louisiana colonial furniture is unending and perhaps one not destined to be fulfilled. Inventories, unknown documents, attics, and secret caches may still lend clues; thus far, however, what is known affords only a sketchy picture. Fires, floods, war, and a lack of appreciation for plantation and locally-made pieces may account for the paucity of existing early Louisiana furniture. That it was French in style, simple in execution, and rich in native woods has been firmly documented. The known examples seem to be from the mid-18th century, continuing until the advent of eastern machine-made furniture in the mid-19th century.

Importing furniture, a modest colonial and early-19th century practice, would be in the late-20th century a relatively new adventure. New Orleans was capable of being self-sufficient in furniture production; it always had a large number of cabinetmakers. The directories and early census list several cabinetmakers from the very founding of the city; in the 1820s and the 1860s hundreds were reported in the city directories.

This forty year period was New Orleans "Golden Era," a time when the port was satisfying the needs of the entire lower Mississippi valley. It was the second major building phase of the city, the first having been accomplished during the mid-colonial period. Plantations flourished, merchants and factors prospered in this city of option, opportunity, and opulence!

The good life—dancing, drinking, gambling—always part of the lifestyle of New Orleans, seduced even its most puritanical newcomers. Scholars submit that interruptions from the good life and the celebration of religious and political holidays fractured and diminished the momentum of business. Others tag the Civil War as the end of that era, and World War II as the marker for revival.

The popularity or longevity of the Seignouret-Mallard furniture may well prove to be financial rather than preferential. After the Civil War and a debilitating Reconstruction Era, the city experienced financial depression. New Orleans neighborhoods stood still, awaiting renewal and expansion, and by then unfashionable interiors yearned for change.

When commerce increased toward the end of the century and money began to flow, many families traded good, handmade 19th century furniture for the more up-to-date machine-made product. Joseph Meeks and Co. from New York had shipped its heavy mahogany tables, buffets, and beds to New Orleans as early as 1840; the market in subsequent years became filled with furniture selections from Michigan, Iowa, and Ohio.

The economic conditions of the city are still echoed within the interiors of New Orleans homes. Early Louisiana furniture is rare, but represented. The "Golden Era" is frozen for review through museum houses. The uptown neighborhoods, experiencing architectural revival, adapt pragmatically. The furniture in most of these mansions, once dark and heavy, now contemplates the future with modern choices of 18th century French and English antiques. The scales of preference seem to tip in favor of the English, and one might conclude that New Orleans, while enjoying the French flavor, has finally become thoroughly American.

NEW ORLEANS NEIGHBORHOODS

LIKE PARIS, New Orleans has its left and right river banks and its collection of faubourgs or neighborhoods. Many are classified in the National Register of Historic Places and have activist organizations to maintain their preservation.

BAYOU ST. JOHN

Faubourg St. John
Faubourg Pontchartrain
Faubourg Jackson

VIEUX CARRE

UPTOWN

Faubourg Ste Marie   *City of Jefferson*
Lower Garden District   *University Section*
Garden District   *City of Carrollton*

DOWNTOWN

Faubourg Marigny
Faubourg Washington

BACK-OF-TOWN

Faubourg Tremé
Faubourg Gueno
Faubourg Allard
Faubourg Gentilly
Faubourg Milne

BAYOU ST. JOHN   As a natural inlet from Lake Pontchartrain, the bayou meanders along a course deep into the present city. Its settlement, in 1708, is the oldest; its brick homes, colonial in type and style, profit climatically by being raised—with high-hipped roofs and deep galleries.

The Pitot House, probably begun by Spanish Don Bartolome Bosque, was completed in 1800 by Frenchman Joseph Reynes. Sold in 1805 to the great-grandmother of French artist Edgar Degas, it was bought in 1810 by James Pitot, first elected mayor of New Orleans. Threatened by demolition in 1962, it was acquired by the Louisiana Landmarks Society and is now a National Historic Landmark, open to the public. The drawing room, opening to both the front and rear galleries, overlooks the bayou. Old Paris vases and a French pasteware finger vase decorate the mantel, carved with lions heads and crossed flags. A Louisiana-made rectangular table with center drawer has cherry legs, a mahogany molded top, and scalloped aprons. The Boutac chair covered in leather is late-18th century; the Sheraton chair and Baltimore inlaid card table are 19th century.

The rear gallery and brick floored loggia of Pitot House reflect a utilitarian function. The mild New Orleans climate permits semi-enclosed open spaces to be incorporated into major living areas. The harvest table is filled with vegetables from a nearby garden (the formal parterred one being in front of the house between the split-cypress fence and the bayou). The chair is of pecan wood with a corn shuck seat. A *sang de boeuf* painted Louisiana armoire contains treenware and household utensils. On the upper gallery, through which breezes pass from the front to the rear, the transomed French doors have a "criss-cross motif" repetitive of that seen in the gallery balustrades.

Further up the bayou, the Sanctuary plantation house majestically faces the water. The simplicity of whitewashed walls and crisply starched bed coverings emphasizes the rich wood tones of the Opelousas-made furniture in this bedroom. A canopied Renaissance revival-style bed with turned posts dominates the room. Nearby a rustic, handmade rocker demonstrates an artisan's creativity through a floret-carved cartouche within its rail back. Two rare pen and ink sketches are by Alexander Drysdale, a New Orleans artist best known for his mass-produced, misty blue and green landscapes. Parts of the house may well have been built in the late 1700s by the well known Spanish colonial Andrés Almonester y Rojas

VIEUX CARRE   The "Old Square" was *Nouvelle Orléans* when founded by Bienville in 1718 as a trading post. Surveyed in 1720, its 18th century rectangular configuration remains but its first buildings have all disappeared. The architecture is primarily 19th century, mostly American with strong influences from the French and the Spanish. Jackson Square, reserved first as the *Place Royalle,* is its center. Two-hundred and twenty-five years of culture is added to the compactness and intimacy of the old town, enhanced by cast and wrought-iron balconies, glimpses of cool patios and unexpected vistas.

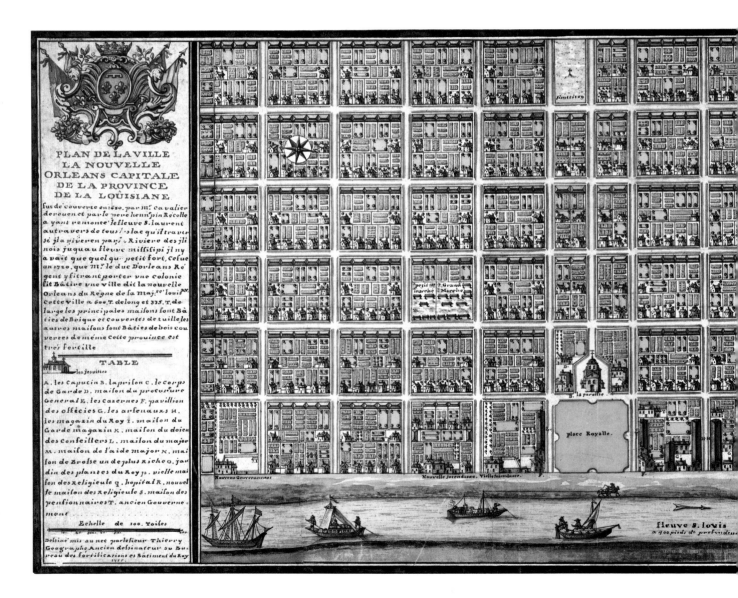

Plan de la Ville la Nouvelle Orleans, Thierry, 1755. Original manuscript map drawn by a French geographer; one of two known to exist. Courtesy of The Historic New Orleans Collection.

The Ursuline Convent is the only surviving building of the French colonial period, and as such is the most historic in New Orleans. Designed by Engineer Ignace François Broutin, it was constructed in 1745 by Claude Villars Dubreuil. The stairway was removed from a still earlier Ursuline convent and installed in this building; the wrought iron is the oldest known local example. The Ursuline nuns, who arrived in New Orleans in 1726 with a group of marriageable young ladies known as the "Casket Girls," had a convent, school, and orphanage here until 1824. The building then became the Bishopric, the rectory for St. Mary's Italian Church, and is now a museum and archives for the New Orleans Archdiocese.

Madame John's Legacy is the earliest building belonging to the Louisiana State Museum and the oldest of its type in the Mississippi Valley. Its name, a fictional one based on the romantic tale "Tite Poulette," by George Washington Cable, is a 19th century appellation. Constructed in 1788, the house has a brick lower level and an upper one of "brick between posts" covered with wide, beaded, horizontal boards. Front and rear galleries have slender columns and segmented doorways. This bedchamber illustrates 18th century Louisiana furnishings, including a canopied four-poster of cherry, a cypress four-post cradle with heavy rockers, a beech slat-back armchair, and a walnut table. The cherry and walnut armoire was made in Vincennes, Indiana, c. 1801; the serpentine-front chestnut chest was probably an import from 18th century Holland.

The Cabildo, once the seat of the Spanish colonial city government, is part of the eight-building complex of the Louisiana State Museum. The marble stairway and heavy walnut balustrade are important remaining elements of the original 1795 structure. It was designed by Gilberto Guillemard, a French architect in the service of Spain. Guarding the main entrance and stair is a bronze cannon called a "Napoleon." Portraits are of Pierre LeMoyne d'Iberville, the French-Canadian who established the Louisiana colonies in 1699, and John Law, the financial genius whose 18th century scheme to settle the colony ended as the "Mississippi Bubble." On the stair landing is a 20th century depiction of the Louisiana Transfer ceremony in the Place d'Armes (Jackson Square).

On the second floor of the Cabildo, in the *Sala Capitular* or Council Chamber, the Louisiana Transfer was signed in 1803. The fireplace wall was removed in 1850 to form a chamber for the Louisiana Supreme Court, but in 1968 this wall was replaced and the room returned to a version of the original. Chairs surrounding the table are Windsor; benches are from the Ursuline Convent. Portraits of personages important to Louisiana history fill the walls. Of particular interest is the full length oil painting, attributed to Spanish colonial painter Salazar, of Don Andrés Almonester y Rojas, who financed the construction of the Cabildo after the fire of 1788. A plaster bust of Thomas Jefferson faces the length of the room, maintaining his eternal approval of the acquisition of the Louisiana territory for the United States.

22

On either side of an original pedimented doorway leading from the enclosed Cabildo gallery are bronze busts of Thomy Lafon and John McDonogh. Lafon, a black philanthropist born in New Orleans in 1810, became one of the richest men in the city and left his entire estate to charity. McDonogh was a merchant and philanthropist whose 1850 will provided funds for the construction of many New Orleans public schools. The adjoining Mayor's Parlor contains an 1816 desk, once the property of Governor Jacques Villeré. The chandeliers, 1805, match those in the Sala Capitular. The mantel dates from 1813 and was removed from the Presbytère when that building was renovated in the 1960s.

The monumental U.S. Mint occupies an entire square at the foot of the Esplanade bordering the Vieux Carré. In colonial times the area was the site of French and Spanish forts, and later served as the bivouac of General Andrew Jackson's small army as it prepared to fight the invading British in 1815. The building was designed in Greek Revival style in 1835 by noted Philadelphia architect William Strickland, and served as a branch mint until 1909. Since then it has been used successively as federal prison, veterans bureau, and Coast Guard station. In 1966 the Mint became the property of the Louisiana State Museum. Extensive renovations were completed in 1980 to preserve the landmark and adapt it for contemporary museum use. One room of the ground level basement is presently unfinished to exhibit the groined arches and 27-inch exterior walls.

Across Jackson Square on its downriver side, the lower Pontalba Building is another State Museum property. Within the row, one unit has been reserved to illustrate the period of its construction and is designated "The 1850 House." A reproduction of a store is on the ground floor, while on the second, the front parlor faces the Square and the dining room overlooks a small interior courtyard. The bedrooms are on the third level; a study, servants rooms, and kitchen occupy a rear attached wing. A large plantation desk in the study and a trunk filled with documents are businesslike accessories, while a French porcelain cup and saucer with blue and gold border indicate a prosperous lifestyle. The cup is stamped "P.Mallard, 67 Royal, New Orleans." Although now known as a cabinetmaker, Mallard advertised as a furniture dealer who stocked glassware. An Old Paris wine jug on the mantel is inscribed "E.F.Mioton & Co. Importers."

Through the full length windows of this upper Pontalba residence, a panoramic view of the heart of the Vieux Carré, Jackson Square, is possible. The Cabildo, Cathedral, Presbytère command the left, while the twin lower Pontalba building may be seen ahead through the trees. Visible from the cast-iron gallery, the river traffic of the Mississippi glides past. Owned by the city, this set of sixteen row houses is rented as stores on the ground floor, and apartments above. Built for the Baroness Micaéla Pontalba in 1850 as a speculative venture, this row, like its mate across the square, were rented as full houses, reaching from the ground floor to attic, including a width of only three windows. The interiors of these buildings have been redistributed; this apartment is the third floor of two former houses. A backgammon table with two Directoire chairs is near Louis XV chairs and depicts a style appropriate to the Francophile ambitions of the baroness.

Standing between the Presbytère and Cabildo, St. Louis Cathedral faces the Mississippi River at Jackson Square. Designed in 1850 by French architect J.N.B. de Pouilly, the building stands on the foundations of two earlier churches. The saga of renovations and redecorations has continued almost every 25 years since its construction, leading to the scene of artistic expression of four major artists working in Louisiana and numerous architects and contractors; the John Geiser family has had three generations of painting contractors embellishing the structure. Pope Paul VI, in 1964, elevated the cathedral to the status of Minor Basilica. A 1975 redecoration resulted in an ivory-white interior, replacing the marbleization and dark colors present since the 1930s. New chandeliers illuminate the original Belgian-made altar of wood and marble beneath the painting of St. Louis, King of France and patron saint of New Orleans.

Casa Hové, a two-level creole house in the Vieux Carré, was built in 1807 by Hilaire Boutet for Valery Nicholas, a glazier and gunsmith. Beaded ceiling beams and original floors enhance the simplicity of the upstairs gallery and bedroom. The bed is attributed to François Seignouret and the armoire to Prudent Mallard, both New Orleans cabinetmakers. In the adjoining drawing room, seen through the glazed casement doors, is a hand-carved box mantel known as the "Honeycomb and Bee." Presently unpainted in the 20th century manner, it is an outstanding design from the early-19th century. An 1834 description provides evidence that the building was utilized as a residence on the upper floor and a "fine store, with corridor and porte cochère on the ground floor." Today a perfumery continues the commercial tradition, and on the second floor, a house museum, the residential one.

In a Joseph Pilié survey of 1818, a creole cottage at the banquette or sidewalk, was depicted with its rear service dependencies. The cottage burned, but the rear building remains, set deep into the narrow lot and now enclosed behind a brick wall and tree-filled garden. The parlor, formerly a kitchen, retains a beamed ceiling from its early period. A bench from the First Presbyterian Church, formerly at Lafayette Square, is a blend of pine, hickory, and oak, with cast-iron arms; the back swings over to allow seating in either direction. Similar to a Shaker design, a small cherry tilt-top table has tripod feet. A Virginia cherry cutting board serves as a coffee table and a classic Acadian cypress table with tapered legs is seen between a Captain's chair and velvet covered Biedermeir-style armchair.

Examples of box or apron mantels similar to this one appear in Vieux Carré creole houses of the early-19th century. This house, probably built by François Dusuau De La Croix in 1810, remained in his family until 1858. The pedestal dining table is set with six pairs of George III silver-gilt fruit forks and knives made in London by Brent and Peppin. A Russian silver-gilt *kovsk* with a horse motif serves as a centerpiece. Silver-plated candelabra on the mahogany serving table bear the touch mark of Matthew Boulton, c. 1810. The K'ang-hsi blue and white plates on 17th century Dutch stands complement the K'ang-hsi ginger jars on 18th century French ormolu bases. The oil painting on canvas above the mantel is in the style of Dutch 19th century painters, and the ''Portrait of a Scholar'' is 17th century Dutch.

The De La Croix House boudoir is swathed in Louis XVI-style Scalamandre silk draperies; the same fabric covers the *chaise longue*. A silk Persian prayer rug in muted shades of green blends with the rich pink and yellow bed draperies of the *lit à la Polonaise*. The shell-shaped chair is an eclectic note within the Directoire theme. An 18th century English portrait hangs above the lovely Dutch chest with marquetry. Two painted chairs Louis XVI-style, are covered in lemon silk. Spode landscape cups rest invitingly next to a Belgian *chocolatière* on a late-18th century French table.

The Beauregard-Keyes House is dedicated to the memory of Confederate General P.G.T. Beauregard, and Frances Parkinson Keyes, author of fifty-one books and its owner from 1944 until her death here in 1970. Built in 1826 by Joseph LeCarpentier, grandfather of chess champion Paul Morphy, it was designed by François Correjolles. Its Federal architecture is atypical and the earliest of its type in New Orleans; only three examples exist in the Vieux Carré. In the Beauregard chamber, seen through the doorway, is a half-tester rosewood bed by Prudent Mallard. The handwoven, silk damask bedspread was once the property of Queen Victoria. In the Louisiana chamber the cherry and cypress armoire, c. 1812, was owned by the Claiborne-Beauregard family. A gondola chair stands near a Canterbury serving table filled with laces of the early-19th century. The house is operated by the Keyes Foundation and is open daily.

Frances Parkinson Keyes wintered in New Orleans. She lived and wrote in the rear service wing while dining and entertaining in this room, an enclosed gallery. The base of the oak table of mid-Victorian period is carved with emblems of the hunt; the chairs and cabinet reveal symbols of plenty. The tea cosy, given to Mrs. Keyes by the Kaiserin Auguste Victoria, wife of Wilhelm II, is handmade and embroidered. A porcelain *veilleuse-théière* (teapot with light) and English china are from the Keyes collection. A large patio and rooftop of the former stable and slave quarters can be seen through the series of double doors which open to the stairway gallery.

With its wide center hall, the Hermann-Grima House is one of the earliest American-style homes in the Vieux Carré. Erected by William Brand in 1831 for Samuel Hermann, a New Orleans merchant, it has a brick façade painted red with white mortar pencilling, in the modish manner of the time. The dining room and parlor, viewed through the rear gallery window, are unified by a period-style patterned carpet. Cypress doors, grained to resemble mahogany and maple, slide through the fluted Corinthian columns and separate the large rooms when closed. Ornate wood carving appears in the parlor in a flower motif and in the dining room as cornucopias of fruit. Furnishings in the parlor show the influence of the French Empire and Restauration periods. The two-story residence, after being the home of the Judge Felix Grima family, became the Christian Woman's Exchange. The house and its dependencies are now a museum designated a National Historic Landmark.

The strength of order and color coordination aids the 20th century viewer in recognizing the cohesiveness of Victorian decorative patterns. The water taffeta draperies and tester, known as lambrequins repeat the green of the floral carpet, a reproduction of a pattern in England's Ashburnam Hall. Prudent Mallard is credited with the design of the rosewood armoire, half-tester bed and dressing table. On the commode next to the bed, a *veilleuse-théière* belonged to Mme Hermann, Jr., née Eugenie DuBuys. The furnishings postdate the Hermann ownership of the house, but could have been present during the Grima residence.

On the ground floor of the three-story service wing of the Hermann-Grima House are the original kitchen and adjacent washroom. In this working kitchen, the restored open hearth fireplace is supplemented by an oven and cooking counter, reconstructed from archeological remnants. Referred to in the building contract as "stew holes," the stove is a typical French *potager*. Pots were placed on tripods or iron grills in or over charcoal fired openings; food could be boiled, fried or braised. Within the large hearth is the movable pot crane and the reflecting oven or tin kitchen, shaped like a half cylinder and equipped with a spit. The ladderback cypress chairs with animal skin seats are typical of those used in simple New Orleans homes and kitchen areas.

La Pharmacie Française, established in 1950, is one of the most significant historical pharmacy museums in the United States. The three and one-half story brick building was designed in 1837 by Jacques de Pouilly for Louis Joseph Dufilho, Jr., as a pharmacy with residence above. Members of the Dufilho family had been licensed apothecaries as early as 1803, an 1816 advertisement in the *Louisiana Courier* placed the "Dufilho Brothers, Apothecaries, on Chartres Street next to the New Exchange Coffee House." The 1870 rosewood cabinets of German manufacture were used in Max Samson's local drugstore until donated to the museum. Along with potions that promise to cure every known ailment and 19th century surgical instruments, there is a marble and onyx soda fountain with brass fixtures from St. Louis ready to dispense soda water and several mineral waters.

Over the cypress mantel, a water color drawing of creole cottages by A. Boyd Cruise depicts the exterior of the cottage of which this dining and living room comprise one-half. The rich, dark tones of the mahogany furniture contrast with the warm glow of unpainted millwork and punkah; the latter is pecan wood, originally painted to resemble oak. The English Regency period and early-19th century are well represented by the tilt-top breakfast table joined by two Regency chairs with striped velour and two William IV mahogany side chairs. Above the sideboard with brass splash rail are Currier and Ives prints of the Battle of New Orleans. A blue and white Chinese rug blends with the blue rough-plaster walls used throughout. A French Restauration bergère is seen near the original box mantel in the living room. This cottage was built in 1824 by Raimond Gaillard, a free person of color, veteran of the Battle of New Orleans, and a prosperous businessman. His heirs owned this home and several other pieces of property in this square until 1861.

In the rear of the Gaillard Cottage are a pair of two-story buildings, originally kitchens below and servants quarters above. Each has been converted to a private apartment. As seen through side windows, framed with blooming confederate jasmine, the small library below doubles as an artist's studio; the Chippendale architect's table has cross-banded edges. Walls surrounding the circular stairway and the bedroom are filled with works of art. The foot of a French Directoire day bed, the top of an oak *prie-dieu*, and the face of a *semainière* (a linen chest with a drawer for each day of the week) can be viewed through the window above. The bedroom opens to a small balcony overlooking the brick courtyard and rear garden.

Gallier House, a National Historic Landmark, is a remarkable
architectural restoration and an accurate recreation of a Louisiana
lifestyle. Designed in 1857 by James Gallier, Jr., for his family, the
house provides an opportunity to review a New Orleans architect's
inventive talents and personal decorative tastes. Gallier, with his
architect father, is credited with some of New Orleans' most
memorable structures. Two of his four daughters shared this
bedroom readied in summer dress for warm weather and
imaginative games. An Old Paris tea set, and copper pots and pans
are period replicas of adult china and utensils. The bed, dresser,
and washstand are eastern-style, pine, cottage furniture with *faux
bois* grained, oddly enough, to resemble pine. Sea grass matting
covered all floors; mosquito netting was a necessity. The tall linen
press of mahogany veneer, c. 1830, has provenance from Mme
Gallier's Louisiana family.

Gallier's floor plans required that a cooking range, a copper boiler, and a sink with hot and cold water be placed in the areas where these appear. The stove, made of cast iron, burns coal and has a maker's mark "T. Hudson's Exors Manchester." The copper boiler is a type shown in an 1866 catalog, and the sink is like ones in other houses designed by Gallier. The original flagstones were relaid, adding another fireproof surface to the room. The walls, which were whitewashed every spring for cleanliness and to "absorb odors," were further brightened by yellow paint trim, layers of which were uncovered by archaeologists working on the restoration, which preceded the opening of the house as a museum in 1971.

Drawings by Gallier, Jr. specified, "bath room hot and cold water and patent water closet and bath tub." In the house restoration, the copperlined walnut tub and the water closet cabinet were copied from an 1866 plumbing catalog; the hot water came from the copper boiler in the kitchen, the cold water from an attic tank. The waste line was made of cast iron and ran to the patio and a 75-inch brick-lined water closet sink. The coal burning fireplace is original. The gas fixture of a hand holding a lily is in the same location as the original. The walnut-veneered *bidet* has a porcelain interior. Walls are covered with marble-patterned wallpaper delineated with grey paint to give a stone-like effect, and the floor is covered in kamptulion, a 19th century version of today's linoleum.

Antoine's Restaurant has achieved worldwide acclaim for New Orleans through its culinary exploits. The St. Louis Street building was constructed as a residence in 1831 and was acquired by Frenchman Antoine Alciatore in 1868. Over the years the restaurant has expanded through a series of connecting buildings, enclosed patios, and service buildings; a mansard roof was added to the main building in 1874. Thematic dining spaces are filled with photographs and historic artifacts. The oval-shaped Rex room epitomizes the city's interest, indeed obsession, with Mardi Gras and those who have helped make it famous. Around the walls are photographs of civic leaders who have held the honor of being Rex, King of the Carnival. Within lighted cases are rhinestone crowns and scepters, ball invitations, and "krewe" favors from years gone by; these are rotated and renewed from the large Mardi Gras resources of The Historic New Orleans Collection.

Past a Victorian door of etched glass and carved wood, visitors enter one of New Orleans small inns. In the Maison de Ville, antiques from Paris, London, and Brussels decorate every room. An 18th century French Provincial chest glistens under an Empire chandelier in the entrance foyer. In the parlor at the end of the hall, a view of the patio and the 18th century service wing is visible. This front building which replaced an earlier structure, was converted to a hotel in the 1950s. One of the former residents of the house was A. A. Peychaud, who is credited with inventing the American cocktail.

Utilized as the reception area of The Historic New Orleans Collection, the Counting House represents a faithful renovation of its 1830s period. Built in 1794, as the rear building of the Merieult House that faces Royal Street, it has evolved from a large warehouse to an elegant Greek Revival room overlooking a lush green patio. The Lizardi brothers purchased the buildings in 1830 and transformed the space into a counting house. The 19th century chandelier of bronze doré with Baccarat prisms is from the Charles Crawford home on Royal Street. At the far end, a painting of the Olivier sisters by Tissier rests above an elaborate gold leaf, marble-topped console with floral motifs. A complex of five connecting buildings houses the collections of General and Mrs. L. Kemper Williams and is open to the public.

A portion of the original Merieult property was demolished in 1889 and replaced by a two-story brick house with rooms opening *ensuite*. In 1938 General and Mrs. Williams purchased the entire complex from Royal to Toulouse Streets and subsequently made the house their residence. Mrs. Williams's bedroom faces the balcony and recessed Toulouse Street patio. Two of six English Regency open arm chairs, japanned, are visible as are a pair of Sheraton writing tables. Early-18th century English chests flank the mantel above which is a water color, "Cybidium," by A. Boyd Cruise, director emeritus of The Historic New Orleans Collection. Among four lithographs by Felix A. B. St. Aulaire of the 1820 period in New Orleans is a rare artist's proof, offered for correction from the famous New Orleans lithographer, Langume.

UPTOWN No fewer than twenty former riverfront plantations and faubourgs were combined into this book's designation of uptown New Orleans. Above or upriver of Canal Street, the land originally was the Bienville Concession. Passing from plantations to Central Business District and five distinct sections each with residences, schools, churches, and businesses, the area is 8½ miles from Canal Street to the Jefferson Parish line. Uptown New Orleanians regard everything downtown and back-of-town as almost out-of-town. Paradoxically, the converse of this attitude was held by 19-century creoles of the Vieux Carré.

St. Patrick's is the oldest church building in New Orleans. Its parish was established in 1833 and the church completed in 1841. Originally designed by Charles and James Dakin as "High Gothic," the foundations of the building faltered and the church trustees hired James Gallier, Sr., to complete the construction. Gallier eliminated many of the exterior Gothic extravagances planned by the Dakins, but unleashed his own lavish inspirations on the interior. The nave and aisles share his display of fan vaulting, with the ribs converging into restrained bosses. The three large paintings by Leon Pomarede above the carved center altar remain some of the finest church canvases of the 19th century. St. Patrick's parishioners have practically disappeared in the residents' exodus from Faubourg Ste Marie, but in 1979 its faithful supporters undertook a five year renovation and restoration program, both interior and exterior.

The New Orleans City Hall from 1850-1952, now called Gallier
Hall in honor of its architect James Gallier, Sr., was built by
Robert Seaton. Facing Lafayette Square, the heart of Faubourg
Ste Marie, it remains one of the best surviving examples of
Greek Revival architecture in the city. The wide central hall
extends the length of the building; a repetitive theme of pilasters
and recessed ceiling panels containing plaster medallions and
dentils forms a strong pattern. Its walls are decorated with
portraits of former mayors. Through the doorway is seen a
carved oak mantel shelf supported by two bronze figures. One
of the former city council chairs is nearby.

The Mayor's parlor overlooking Lafayette Square is furnished with the original city purchases of American Victorian pieces of carved rosewood and mahogany. A portrait of General Andrew Jackson is reflected in the mantel mirror, and that of James H. Caldwell, the father of gas lighting in New Orleans and major developer in this American Sector, hangs above the Steinway grand piano. The crystal and bronze doré chandelier is original to the room. Recessed ceiling panels repeat the pattern introduced in the hallway, with the proportion of the center panel and size of the medallion adjusted to the grandeur of the room. Saved by the efforts of the Louisiana Landmarks Society in 1950, the building is used for receptions, meetings and Mardi Gras festivities.

Within the architectural inventory of the Friends of the Cabildo book, *New Orleans Architecture, The American Sector*, ''Marble Hall'' in the U.S. Custom House, 1848-1881, is described ''. . . one of the finest Greek Revival interiors in America. It measures 125 feet by 95 feet and is 54 feet high. The ceiling is of ground glass, with a stained glass border, above which a skylight admits an abundance of illumination; the ceiling is supported by 14 marble columns, the capital of each embellished with reliefs of Juno and Mercury. Above the door at the N. Peters end of the hall are two panels containing life-size bas-reliefs of Bienville and General Andrew Jackson. Between them is a pelican feeding her young, the emblem of Louisiana, created by local sculptor A. Defrasse. The hall floor is of black and white marble, set with circular disks of heavy glass, through which light is admitted to the engine rooms beneath.'' Alexander T. Wood was the first of five architects and engineers to design and work on the building during its many years of construction.

Characteristic of Faubourg Ste Marie is the brick side-hall townhouse now serving as a law office. Built in 1848, its parlors and patios, woodwork and cornices have been preserved. The original floor of wide pine boards had disappeared; pink Belgian slate replaces it in the firm's boardroom. The brass and copper light fixture with anthemion motif has strong direct lines as do the tables and leather upholstered chairs. All are early-20th century pieces. Two of the paintings represent New Orleans architectural scenes; an oil, done in a style popularized during the Works Progress Administration is above the original marble mantel. The restoration received a Chamber of Commerce Award in 1973 as the most outstanding remodeling of a small building in the Central Business District.

Within a pair of 1834 buildings is the sunlit office of a young investment counselor. A tree-filled patio below affords this building rare open space within the Central Business District, Faubourg Ste Marie. Millwork is of the period of the building. The late-19th century stretcher-based table with a Chippendale chair, faces two Windsor chairs with crescent stretchers. Across the room, along the wall of exposed brick is an 18th-century French fruitwood server. The two buildings are excellent examples of New Orleans building by analogy; that is, incorporating architectural features popular from one building to another.

The history of the First National Bank of Commerce is the history of
banking in 19th century New Orleans. Its predecessor, the New
Orleans Canal and Banking Co., was granted a charter to build the
New Basin Canal in 1831. With the completion of its chartered task,
it survived panics, pestilences, and war, and by the early 1900s had
absorbed ten other banks. In 1927 Emile Weil designed this
eighteen story building, said to have the fortress-like strength of a
Florentine palazzo. This plastered ceiling with hexagonal coffers is
richly filled with floral bosses, paterae, dentils, and rope designs. A
band of guilloche, fretwork, and modillions completes the pattern
as the ceiling meets the arcaded walls. Marble pilasters with
Corinthian capitals orchestrate a vertical beat. The massive scale
and detail of this great banking hall demonstrate Weil's ability to
work ancient themes into modern requirements.

Lower Garden District

As a major 19th century work, St. Mary's Assumption Church is deserving of its listing as a National Historic Landmark. Under construction from 1858 to 1860, its Baroque style captures the architectural preferences of the German-American Roman Catholic congregation it was designed to serve. Strength is implicit in the exterior brickwork displaying virtuosity of corbeling and molding, and in the interior emphasis on color, form, and proportions. Deeply grooved pilasters and columns support stylized Corinthian capitals, while waves of bold ribbing form a dramatic ceiling pattern. The altar came to New Orleans in 1874 from the world-renowned Mayers Institute in Munich. At the turn of the century, rows of exposed light bulbs were installed to outline the main altar. The dark carved choir loft with heavy bosses and matching confessionals gleam in their reflected light.

Facing Coliseum Square in the Lower Garden
District, the Strachan House was built in the
late 1840s as a large side-hall double-galleried
brick home. The furnishings represent the
union of heirlooms from Virginia, Georgia,
Arkansas, and New Orleans. Of thirty-six
lyre-back chairs, fashioned locally for the St.
Louis Cathedral, these are two of eight known
to survive. The owner's interest in Napoleon is
evident in several colored lithographs of the
General and the rare book on the library table,
titled *Campaignes de Napoleon, Primier*, published in Paris in 1806. An Atwater Kent 1927
radio sits between the front windows.

On the former Rousseau Plantation within
Faubourg Lafayette, Henry Howard designed
this large frame house with an attached
servants' wing for Manuel Goldsmith. The
original 1860 frescoes may have been the work
of P. Gauldi, who was working for Howard at
this time, or of Dominic Canova. Alan Sheen,
the present owner, has decorated the house
with family heirlooms and period antiques. The
Italian Renaissance hall table is a fourth generation family piece. The stair railing of Cuban
mahogany and the spindles of a tulip design are
Howard favorites.

Beneath the vibrant Pompeian frescoes of the Goldsmith-Sheen House, David Fischer, one of New Orleans first impresarios, entertained such international guests, as Galli-Curci, Nijinsky, Caruso, and John McCormick. Within this ballroom, the original marble mantels, graceful gilded arch, and ceiling medallions remain. The piano, made in London between 1800 and 1810, is an Erard; the music stand is Spanish. Chairs lining the walls are Hepplewhite, 1770, and the two tables are Chippendale, 1760, and George II. Chandeliers throughout the house are 17th century-style Venetian with a daffodil design.

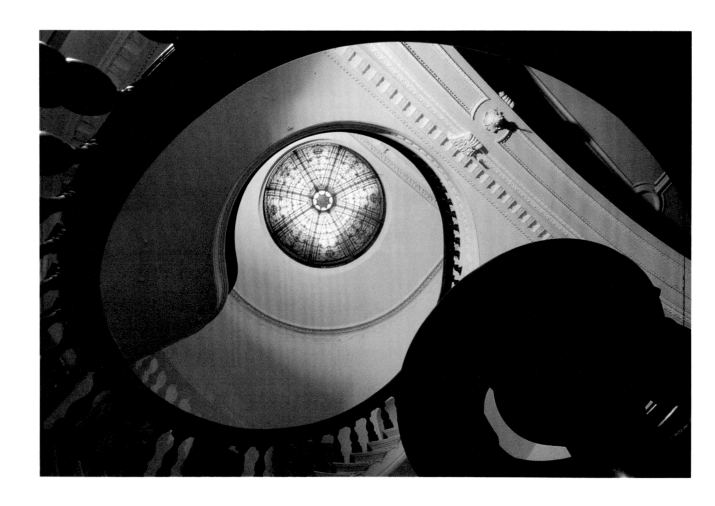

Garden District

A golden light floods the mahogany stairway of the Louise S. McGehee School from the stained glass domelight three stories above the marble-floored hall. By tradition, this Garden District building with its superb Beaux Arts interior is credited to James Freret, a New Orleans architect who studied in France. It was constructed in 1872 as a residence for sugar planter Bradish Johnson, at a reputed cost of $100,000. Although the building has served as a girls' private school since 1929, its architectural features remain intact. By coincidence, an earlier cottage on the site housed, in the 1860s, the Carnatz Institute, "a fashionable academy for young ladies."

Architectural features of this raised cottage in Faubourg Livaudais indicate that it may have been
built as early as 1833. Known to have been requisitioned during the Civil War, it has been in the
possession of the same family for 55 years. Marble mantels replace wooden ones; otherwise, the
two rooms retain their original simplicity. The 1870 portrait above the mahogany serving table is of
Sarah Eleonore Carroll of Virginia, whose silver epergne graces the round oak pedestal table
beneath a German silver chandelier. On the mantel is a silver loving cup from the Louisiana Club,
and above is the ancestral portrait of a Canadian clergyman. A pair of carved rosewood side chairs
are from Houmas Plantation on the River Road. In the library the walnut bookcases were made for
St. Paul's rectory. A mahogany card table, probably Louisiana-made, is from Natchitoches.

Sometime between 1838 and 1842, Thomas
Toby, a Philadelphia-born commission merchant, built this galleried raised plantation-
style house in Faubourg Lavandais. His widow
sold it to Thomas Dugan whose descendants
continue to own and occupy the comfortable
home. This room was once an open gallery
delightfully described in 1875 by Dugan's
daughter: "The back gallery was 'awned' and
[the] floor covered. Brackets with ivy, and
flower stands in every corner and the parlor
windows opening out on it. Part of the long
gallery was also 'awned' and [the] rest shut
out by a large flower stand." Now enclosed, it
serves as a dining room, furnished with 19th
century pieces which include a Louisiana
armoire, now a *verrier.* Through the French
doors may be seen the new gallery and a part
of the spacious, tree-filled grounds surrounding the house.

Built in 1866, this house also became part of the Newcomb Music School and Baptist Bible Institute. When lovingly restored by the present owners, it was discovered that like its twin, the Richardson House, it was constructed of cypress with random-width pine floors, all morticed and tenoned, and hand-made with square nails. The long side hall gives easy access to the parlor, library, and dining room. Within the latter, the table is Louisiana-made, 1835; the chairs, Chippendale, 1790. The epergne carries the marks of silver-smith Matthew Boulton, and the 1840 Bristol and Waterford chandelier is from the Jesuit Retreat House in Mississippi. Walls of the room are lined with Ellsworth Woodward paintings. The hardware and splash of the Regency sideboard are original. The black and gold Austrian marble mantel with cast-iron frame work is from a New Orleans house designed by Henry Howard. Parlor and library mantels (not visible) are from the demolished Uncle Sam's Plantation.

The Richardson House, built between 1866 and 1868, became in the early-20th century part of the Newcomb Music School and later the Baptist Bible Institute. Purchased in 1954 by the present owners, it has been returned to a gracious residence. The exterior of the frame building is restrained, even its dining room bay is but a modest protrusion. Dining table, chairs, and breakfront were made for the room by Manheim Galleries of New Orleans. The mahogany card table with ormolu is American Empire. A Kerman rug covers random-width pine boards. The house is listed on the register of the Historic House Association.

A bronze marker introduces passers-by to this center-hall house with its unusual curved side gallery: "Adams-Jones House erected for John I. Adams, Merchant, who in 1860 purchased this part of the former plantation of Jacques François de Livaudais, built this house and made his residence here until 1896 . . . restored 1961-62 by Mrs. Hamilton Polk Jones." Through tall dining room doors can be seen a portion of the drawing room and past it the magnificent blue sitting room facing the front garden. Crystal chandeliers and marbleized baseboards enrich each, but it is only in the dining room that double bands of decorated plaster molding are evident above walls covered with 18th century French "water nymph" wallpaper. The elaborately carved Chippendale wall server displays an early-18th century family silver service and Regency candelabra. Over the original marble mantel is a family portrait by the French artist Jean Vaudechamp who worked in Louisiana. Pompeian reds of the Herez rug combine with those of the velvet chair covers and wallpaper border.

Within the Adams-Jones House, all the tall doors are of cedar, grained to resemble mahogany; the knobs and hinges are of silver plate over brass. The 1840 crystal chandelier from Perry, England, dominates not only the center hall with its mahogany stairway, but the adjoining drawing room. Here the George II sofa is covered by gros and petit point needlework depicting a scene of arcadian pleasures. The walls of the drawing room are painted the same soft peach seen in the petit point tapestry.

This small salon in the Adams-Jones House is best described as a chinoiserie fantasy with rococo touches. Against the wall is a giltwood console table attributed to Thomas Johnson, whose theme is from Aesop's fables—*The Wolf in Sheep's Clothing.* The mantelpiece of Scottish pine emphasizes the English absorption of French Rocaille decoration often utilized by designers Ince and Mayhew. The wallpaper is a reproduction of an 18th century pattern from Gracie and Co. The chairs and sofa are the design of Josef Hoffmann, an early mover of the Art Deco period and co-founder of the Viennese Workshop. The double-tester bed seen through the door is one of the finest 18th century Philadelphia-made beds in the country.

A guide to early architecture in New Orleans described this Garden District house as "a fine, small, two-story house with cast-iron galleries, ascribed to Robert D. Boutcher, architect-builder, in 1864." The drawing room of the side-hall residence was added in 1965. In contrast to the simple classic architectural features of the house, the room is embellished with French furnishings. The Louis XVI salon suite is signed Gailliard. The kingwood, kidney-shaped writing table is transitional Louis XV-XVI, while mahogany tables on either side of the couch are pure Louis XVI. A French clock of white marble and bronze gilt adorns the mantel. The latter, found locally, repeats the "Greek Key" design of the double-doors molding; Meissen plates, c. 1770, decorate its shelf. The surrealist painting and pencil sketches are by a modern New Orleans artist, Gary Hoover. All chandeliers are Austrian, late-18th century. In the second parlor near two French Consulat armchairs signed "Jacob D. Frères-R. Meslée," is a Louis XVI, fruitwood and mahogany, ormolu-mounted desk with fire screen.

A cast-iron gateway leads past a luxuriant garden to the gracious entrance of this Garden District home, resplendent with architectural features of the 1850s. Double full length windows were placed at each end of the parlors to allow for cross ventilation and passage to the galleries. A triple elliptical arch with elaborate bosses, consoles, and keystone satyr define these rooms. Twin gold leaf mirrors above the original marble mantels reflect light from the Waterford crystal chandeliers, and create the illusion of width in the rooms measuring 18 by 40 feet with 14 foot ceilings. A superb collection of Chinese porcelains adorns the 18th century English furniture.

This library was originally the double parlor of a side-hall residence built in 1857 on the ''Avenue'' portion of the Faubourg Livaudais. Over the years the once simple house, has been considerably embellished both inside and out to display changing tastes. Nineteenth century portraits, one of Mme Fleitas and one of William C. C. Claiborne, Jr., son of the first American governor, represent the amalgamation of ancient French and Spanish families in New Orleans, and the introduction of Virginia ancestry. The 18th century English desk, with olive wood lamps blends with a 19th century English daybed sofa and with the gros and petit point covered Louis XV style arm chairs. The drawing room, which spreads the width of the house, is filled with delicate, New Orleans-made Louis Philippe pieces, now painted to create harmony with Directoire chairs and an exquisite French marquetry cabinet next to the Louis XVI marble mantel.

The gold tones of the Maddox-Brennan House drawing room are repeated in the present living room, formerly the library, and in the dining room. Whereas the ceiling molding in these two rooms is simple in contrast to the "double transparencies" (open-work plaster moldings set out from the wall at a slight angle) in the center hall, it is the proportions of the doors and windows and the quality of their "Greek Key" (crossette) architraves that give these rooms great elegance. The living room mantel (not visible) is of burl walnut as is the beautiful set of sliding doors. Furnishings, including the 1790 mahogany and satinwood sideboard are English.

→

The interiors of many Garden District-Faubourg Livaudais homes are more elaborate than their exteriors. Serenity is the keynote to the exterior of the Maddox-Brennan House, with its broad, columned galleries. Designed in 1852 by local architect John Barnett, it was built for Joseph Maddox. The ceilings of the gold drawing rooms are covered in a wood-block wallpaper, probably French and installed by the celebrated late-19th century Siebrecht Company. Restored by muralist Vera Reinike, after being damaged by smoke in a 1954 fire, the three borders are separated by delicate gold reed molding. The ornate gilded Corinthian capitals, medallions, and center arch are typical of the extroverted decorative preferences of the mid-to-late-19th century. The diagonally laid oak floor also creates a dramatic effect.

Henry Howard was one of New Orleans most prolific 19th century architects. Since so many of his buildings remain, time has treated his memory and edifices kindly. The masonry, Italianate mansion designed by him for Colonel Robert Henry Short in 1859 and constructed by Robert Huyghe, continues to display Howard's skills. A series of sliding doors and double archways are in detailed but controlled Greek and Roman Revival styles. Their monumentality and that of the spaces they divide provide pleasure to the architectural voyeur. The crystal chandelier, moved from the center hall, is original to the house; furniture throughout is 19th century French. Fortuny fabrics draped in the 19th century manner adorn windows and gallery doorways. The property is enclosed by a cast-iron fence with the famous "corn stalk and morning glory" design, furnished by Wood and Miltenberger of Philadelphia and New Orleans.

George Washington Cable, a 19th century author of national fame, once owned and resided within an entire square of Faubourg Livaudais. His property was subdivided by the late 1880s, and was soon filled with galleried cottages. The parlor of this one is a treasury of Louisiana furniture. Three tables are excellent pieces of walnut, joined and pegged with a provenance from the Ursuline Convent. Along the wall, between the sunlit windows, one of a pair of tables has a curved apron and legs. The table in front of the sofa has "cloven-hoof" feet whereas the smaller table has "hoof" feet and saltire stretchers. The upholstered chair with restrained cabriole legs is of red bay, a wood used in 18th century Louisiana furniture. The bookcase is a mid-19th century cherry piece from Kentucky. Visible in the dining room is a table having tapered legs, of tulip poplar with a Louisiana provenance.

A bedroom within the Cable Square cottage displays additional pieces of extremely fine Louisiana furniture. The cherry armoire is inlaid with a series of paterae under the cornice. On its doors, ovals within rectangles of stringing complete the sophisticated embellishments. The cornice, also banded by lines of double inlay, repeats the deftly worked inlay in the scalloped apron; cabriole legs and fische hinges are further indicators of its early date. The simpler commodes on either side of the bed are also of cherry; lamps are cherry bedpost finials. The Renaissance Revival convent bed from Opelousas, Louisiana is 1870 period, and machine-made.

The Garden District has many rows of shotgun houses, both double and single, some ornately Victorian, with heavy porch brackets; others plain, in the Greek Revival style. Pictured is a home built in the 1870s as part of a speculative development romantically called ''Bride's Row'' or the ''Seven Houses of the Seven Sisters.'' Modernizing the shotguns, and placing antiques of preference, rather than locally available, has been fashionable for the past thirty years. Here the owner has an English, late-19th century breakfront, Chippendale-style claw-foot chairs, accents of Imari porcelain, and Japanese paintings below French Empire wall sconces. The mantel vases, filled with aromatic eucalyptus, are Austrian, and the Kashmir rugs were specially woven for the house.

Facing the Grand Cours Wiltz, this raised center-hall house is brick with a deep gallery. Constructed in 1866, its strong decorative elements introduce Italianate segmentally arched windows. The dining room retains its original bronze ''pulley'' chandelier. A three pedestal, 18th century-English table is surrounded by Louisiana-made mahogany chairs. Oriental porcelains and roof tiles accent the mantel and table. A Regency bench joins the rooms. A Portuguese handwoven wool rug repeats a pattern from the Victoria and Albert museum; the living room Oushak continues the muted shades.

Original wall stencils continue the reds, golds, and greens from the parlor of the Freret House into the center hall that connects the front and rear galleries. The purple brocaded Victorian sofa and chair are Louisiana-made, and the gold-leaf swan sofa is a Russian Empire piece. Richness of color is repeated in the strong tones of the oriental and turkish rugs.

George Purves probably designed this Louisiana plantation-style house in 1856, for James P. Freret, a prominent cotton broker whose young son James, Jr., was himself destined to become an outstanding architect. Built immediately upriver of the Garden District in Faubourg Wiltz, later, Delassize, the house has spacious galleries around three sides. The front parlor and salon both have matching Louis XVI bronze doré chandeliers and twin over-mantel mirrors. A pair of American Federal sofas with cane, a Boulle book case, and a Louis Napoleon console are complemented by signed Jacob Frères chairs and salon sofa. The plaster medallions and cornices are defined in pastel shades.

Importer Henry Rice purchased an entire city square, carved from the former Delachaise plantation. In 1866 he built the Italianate raised villa in which this spiral stairway is an important architectural feature. Rising from the ground floor to the third, it joins the large house vertically, while a wide central hallway unifies access horizontally. The stair's massive finial posts and outstanding molded handrail balance the delicacy of its circular movement. For ninety-eight years this house, with two added brick wings, was the Fink Asylum, a Protestant home for widows. Again a private residence, detached from the rear wings, the Rice House was selected for the National Register in 1977.

The neighborhood bar or saloon has for generations been a social center within both the local black and white communities. In Faubourg Delassize, a building of three stories with a pressed tin ceiling and cast-iron façade was built in 1880 as a furniture store. It became a drugstore in 1899 and served as such for the next fifty years. When restored in the 1970s the golden oak gridwork, pressed tin ceiling, and original bar made it a perfect setting for its neighborhood. A poster of May Irvin, noted American opera star, joins pharmaceutical and cigar advertisements recalling the original function of the building. Light fixtures are from a demolished New Orleans convent; a handsome lamp seen in the foreground, stamped "Fabrication Français," is Moorish and has a shade inlaid with red and green stones.

City of Jefferson

The living room of this late-19th century house in Faubourg
Bouligny radiates expertise in the selection of exquisite porcelains,
paintings, and furniture. Reading from left to right and backward,
the sofa, a *corbeille* is Louis XVI; chairs, Restauration period are next
to painted Italian chairs; both sets are Directoire-style. On the
bookcase are French shepherd "squeezies" or late-18th century
plaster proofs squeezed from a mold. Two Chinnery-type paintings
flank the carved mantel from Avignon. An Agra rug coordinates
the whole and leads to a significant number of French treasures in
the dining room.

A knee hole desk and a low boy, both walnut and George II, are on either side of the 18th century English bed. A mid-18th century oak cricket table and corner chair is near a George II high boy. A demolished bishopric in Marseilles yielded the lovely pair of closet doors, and Nièvre, France, the 17th century Nevers faïence plaques. An over-door painting, fragments of Jacobite embroidery, and Chinese reverse paintings ornament the walls. The 19th century is represented by the Persian camel's hair rug and the Dutch chandelier based on a 17th century style.

The Benjamin C. Toledano House in Rickerville
typifies the area's commodious homes, and
reflects influences of England's Aesthetic movement. The oriental style of the bedroom became
popular in America through New York furniture
makers, emanating from Anglo-Japanese designs
by E. W. Godwin, an English architect and
designer. The golden maple of the twin beds,
dressing table, mirror, and plant stand was
turned and grained to resemble bamboo. Appointments to please little girls are a miniature
Old Paris tea set, Bébè Jumeau and Floradora
dolls, and Bye Low babies in antique dresses. The
painting of the child in white is a family portrait
signed by Achille Peretti, c. 1850.

University Section

The three block width of Hurstville stretches from the Mississippi River to Claiborne Avenue and is named for Cornelius Hurst, a cotton factor. The area, like neighboring Rickerville, developed in the 1880s and 1890s. Incised moldings, the overmantel, and the use of decorative tiles around the fireplace are superb examples of an interpretative Eastlake interior. The wooden hat rack and settee were purchased for the house in 1906 on a honeymoon trip to Switzerland by the parents of the present owner.

◄ Judah P. Benjamin, the great New Orleans jurist and statesman, was also an important planter-businessman. With his parents he came to New Orleans in 1818, was admitted to the bar in 1832, and elected U.S. Senator in 1852 and again in 1859. Although opposed to slavery and secession he became the Confederacy's Secretary of State and was regarded as its most brilliant leader. This center-hall house in Hurstville was purchased by him in 1853. It was confiscated by federal troops in 1862 and was never again to be occupied by him or members of his family. Probably built in the late 1840s the house was moved from the center of the square facing St. Charles to its present position. A slightly raised cottage, it represents, in the once rural area, a popular house type. Gothic chairs are late-19th century but the card tables are of the period of the house. The dining room set was made by New Orleans cabinetmaker, Joseph Bruno.

City of Carrollton

In 1871, following the loss of her plantation after the Civil War, Mrs. Carolyn Pierce Hoey built a simple barge-board cottage in Carrollton. In its parlor she placed many furnishings from her former, more spacious home. An exquisitely carved card table, Parisian dessert plates, fine crystal and rare books, contrast with a branding iron, now used as a fireplace poker and a brass school bell. All give evidence of the plantation lifestyle. The mahogany armoire, by a Louisiana cabinetmaker is unusual in having corner columns that swing with the doors. Situated only twelve blocks from the site of Hoeyville Plantation, the cottage is owned and occupied by a fourth generation Hoey.

This wide and luxurious center hall exemplifies architectural and furniture fashions popular to Esplanade Ridge homes in the late 19th century. Originally built in 1832 as a Georgian-style building, the house has undergone several changes. Elaborate alterations occurred inside when ornate plaster arches, consoles, and wallpaper were installed. The dining room "pulley" chandelier of brass and pewter is a twin to the one in the hall. The Elizabethan revival, carved oak furniture c. 1870-1880, the hall table, and dining room chairs were imported from Switzerland and are in harmony with the Renaissance revival bookcase on the right. An American Empire sofa, c. 1830, may be a Philadelphia piece. Velvet *portières* are a typical feature of late-19th century interiors as is the wallpaper. The grandson of Louisiana's first American Governor William C. C. Claiborne purchased this house in 1894; his descendants continue to occupy it.

DOWNTOWN In 1834, thirty-four plantations narrowed to the river's edge in only 3¼ miles to form the downtown section of New Orleans. These lands now fan out toward Lake Pontchartrain and include 20th century developments. With the exception of Faubourg Marigny, splendidly built up by 1840, most of downtown along the river is densely populated with late-19th century shotguns, camelbacks and creole cottage rows.

Within this unusual cottage triplex, possibly built as early as 1836, each section is three rooms deep with common walls under a single roof. The façade is rusticated masonry, now painted and pencilled. The parlor contains a Charles X-style sofa of mahogany trimmed with ormolu and gilt. Less ornate southern pieces include an 1820s walnut armoire from Hessmer, Louisiana. A late-18th century French ladderback armchair complements the collection of Louisiana walnut ladderbacks and dining table, c. 1820. A succession of transomed doors leads to a kitchen with stairway, the wall of which curves gently upward exemplifying the fine carpentry skills employed in these modest Faubourg Marigny houses. Called the Nathan-Cizek House it has been owned by prosperous free people of color and was possibly built for a Jewish merchant, Asher W. Nathan.

BACK-OF-TOWN Behind the Vieux Carré, as far back as Bayou St. John and along the east and west boundaries of Lake Pontchartrain, much of the land settlement predates that of the old city. It contains the roads to the bayous *(les Chemins du Bayou, de la Metairie, du Sauvage)*, ancient high roads that led through a series of flooded areas. A 19th-century visitor, Berquin-Duvallon, wrote: "It was . . . the Bayou Road which led from the back of the town to the cantons of Gentilly, Metairie, Grand Bayou . . . which was the link with Bayou Saint Jean and Lake Pontchartrain." In 1810 a large parcel was sold to the city by Claude Tremé; this and Faubourgs Gueno, Gentilly, Allard and Milne are, along with the Bayou St. John faubourgs, considered back-of-the-town.

As seen through the doorways of adjoining double parlors, a serpentine walnut stairway dominates the hall alcove with its graceful upward sweep. The bleached cypress caryatids were purchased by the owner in the 1960s from D. H. Holmes, New Orleans' oldest "emporium." The flamboyantly decorative arch rests on two wall brackets and crosses the space displaying plaster flowers, ropes, egg and dart motifs, and acanthus leaves. This Esplanade Ridge dwelling, built in 1873 by George Washington Dunbar, remains one of the few surviving mansard houses in New Orleans.

In Faubourg Tremé or "back of town," a galleried creole cottage remains close to architectural purity. Charles Martinez, a free man of color, commissioned his father-in-law, Pierre Olivier, and François Muro, both free persons of color, to construct a *maison principale* in 1841. This dormered "brick-between-posts" cottage is two rooms deep with a single *cabinet* under which is a tiny *cave*, a cool, ground-level, dirt-floored space for food and wine storage. Covering the exterior are "bleached battens lap-jointed with hidden nails. . . ." Deeply recessed in its acre of land, the cottage is contained within lush plantings of nandina, azaleas and banana trees. The original dining room mantel is adorned with 18th century salt glazed dishes and Meissen birds; an 18th century English hunt scene fits comfortably above. The ladderback chairs with rush seats, the starched lace table cloth, and small creamware tureen are true to the period of the house.

The Audler-Whitecloud creole cottage, in Faubourg Gueno, built in the late-1830s was moved within its square. Its exterior exhibits 20th century changes but its interior retains a four-room plan, *faux bois* doors, and multi-colored molding. Louisiana armoires, tables and chairs of superb quality are throughout. The library armoire is one of three documented early-19th century ones of this type. The small tapered leg table is of cherry with cypress; the framed sampler is signed Maria Marchand, New Orleans, 1813. A second armoire, in the family room, is late-18th century, of walnut with cabriole legs, a scalloped apron and paneled doors.

New Orleans Museum of Art is housed in a neoclassic-style building on land that was the former Allard Plantation bordered by Bayous St. John and Metairie. Presently it is part of City Park, one of the largest municipal parks in the south and one planned by the designers of New York's Central Park. From a contest of fifty-nine architects, the plans of Chicago firm Lebenbaum and Marx were chosen. New Orleanian Julius Koch was the contractor. Built in 1910 it was the first building constructed in the south as a museum. Isaac Delgado, a New Orleans philanthropist donated $150,000 and his art collection to the project; until recently it was known as Delgado Art Museum. The central court, with mosaic tile floor, surrounded by fluted Ionic columns, continues as excellent exhibition space.

Set within eight acres of formal and picturesque gardens, Longue Vue House was designed in 1939 by New York architect, William Platt, for the Edgar B. Stern family. Classical in style, it follows a symmetrical plan with wings extending from each side. The central section of the interior contains a sweeping three-level staircase surmounted by a domed skylight. The components of this lovely stair typify the exceptionally fine millwork throughout. The second level, divided by double pairs of fluted Ionic columns repeats the architectural symmetry. Here panoramic wallpaper depicting the city of Lyons was block printed in 1823 by Felix Sauvinet. The Anglo-Irish blown glass chandelier, English hanging lanterns, etched glass sconces, and fine inlaid Baltimore table highlight the excellent 18th and 19th century English and American antiques predominating in the house. It is through the generosity of Mrs. Edith Stern that the Longue Vue Foundation was established to make this magnificent house, its collections and gardens available for touring.

An entwined "AP" represents the union of
Micaëla Almonester and Joseph Delfau de Pontalba.
It serves as a monogram in the graceful cast-iron
railing of the Pontalba Buildings.

The Friends of the Cabildo express their sincere thanks to Samuel Wilson, Jr. and Mary Louise Christovich; to Louisiana State Museum Director Robert R. Macdonald, Historic New Orleans Collection Director Stanton M. Frazar and to the members of their staffs; and particularly to Ann Gunderson Conroy, Lydia Huggins, Benjamin W. Yancey, Patricia B. Rittiner, and Kathryn Webster Barnett. The Friends also gratefully acknowledge the cooperation of the many persons and institutions who opened their properties, furnished information, and graciously allowed photographs. The watercolor drawings that appear in the Introduction are from the New Orleans Notarial Archives and can be found in Plan Book 82, Folio 19; Plan Book 97, Folio 19; Notary L. T. Caire, Vol. 85, Act 219; Notary E. Barnett, Vol. 64, Act 444; Notary C. Brown, Vol. 1, Act 93. All the proceeds of the book are donated to the Louisiana State Museum.